This book is dedicated to my

My children, Amber and Jake.

Thank you for coming into to my world and reminding me how to be a child again, to love unconditionally and to be a better person.

To my husband Pete, my inspiration, my soul mate and my best friend. I will love you for eternity.

To my Mum and Dad, who are not only my parents, but my friends.

Thank you for nurturing my creative soul, for making me strong, happy and independent.

It is because of you, I have a lust for life, a thirst for knowledge and a hunger for experience.

Your unconditional love has given me the ability to see the good in all people and for this, I will be forever grateful. I love you both so much.

Sarah x

The Mirror (written aged 15)

The mirror shows me what I am,
But conveniently lies.
For the face I see in front of me,
Is simply a disguise.
It covers all my worries,
Conceals my constant fears.
It gives no clue to how I feel,
A smile confronts my tears.
Perhaps if I knew who I was
And the disguise was took away.
I could deal with all my worries
And live life day by day.
But I'm trapped within my outer self.
Feelings hold me still.
Perhaps one day I'll see myself?
Perhaps I never will?

The Actor (written aged 34)

I gaze at my reflection,
The image isn't whole.
It's simply an illusion.
It can't display my soul.
For this is who I truly am
And who I've always been.
The mirror shows an actor,
Performing in a dream.
I'm happy with my character,
I play a splendid role.
The journey that I'm sticking to
Does not forsake my soul.
Each day I live, I laugh and love.
And sometimes, just create.
I've come to learn, my every thought
Will help to carve my fate.
I'm starting to remember.
No longer in a void,
I am pure consciousness
And cannot be destroyed.
I gaze at my reflection
And see a knowing smile.
The actors face is finite.
Life only lasts a while.
But now I understand it.
Finally, I see,
That I am part of everything.
And it is part of me.

The Stars

Upon the stars I cast my gaze,
Spectators of a billion days.
As seasons come and seasons go,
I wonder why? Perhaps they know?
What if their ancient eyes could see,
Beyond our world great mysteries?
I think that they would understand,
Why Autumn leaves will touch the land,
Why dawn will break the darkest night
And love will shine the brightest night.

Inner Sat-nav

Listen to your heart,
It's the sat-nav for your soul.
If you're on the road to nowhere,
It will show you where to go.

Listen to your heart,
It's the gateway to your dreams.
If your thoughts are a distraction,
And you're broken at the seams...

Listen to your heart,
It will light the path ahead.
Your mind will see the easy road,
Take the path instead.

Your heart knows where it's going,
It's really very clever.
Your destinations 'Happiness',
In a town they call 'Forever'.

Think Big Thoughts

The more you think,
The more you'll see.
The more you see,
The more you'll be.
The more you be,
The more you'll know.
The more you know,
The more you'll grow.
The more you grow,
The more you'll give.
The more you give,
The more you'll live.
The more you live,
The more you'll smile.
So think big thoughts once in a while.

Flimby by the Sea

I've often heard our village,
Called 'Flimby by the Sea.'
They say it with a knowing smile
And local irony.

For Flimby's homes aren't made of slate.
There's no Keswican frills.
There are no trees beside a lake
For Wordsworth's daffodils.

But look again and you will find,
That Flimby's secret gleams,
Beneath its simple structure
And its grey, imperfect seams.

Where countryside meets coastline,
Where water greets the earth.
A haven overlooking,
The majestic Solway Firth.

Have you seen the view to Criffel,
On a clear and sunny day?
And the golden, ember sunsets,
That can take your breath away?

You can take a walk down Pennygill,
Or through the woods at dusk.
Where the essence of wild garlic,
Gives the air a fragrant musk.

And the deeper in the woods you go,
The more you're sure to see.
A secret cave, a hidden pond,
An old enchanted tree.

If you keep your windows open,
You'll hear the magic sound,
Of the music from the ice cream van
As it makes its daily round.

There's a play park for the children.
Train station and bus stop.
A village school, a hair salon,
A post and paper shop.

But the jewel in Flimby's rural crown,
Is its community.
A sentiment of olden days
And local unity.

For Flimby folk are full of life.
And like to solve their quarrels.
Keep open minds, don't judge their own,
Uphold their views and morals.

And in this crazy, mixed up world,
We know we've got it good.
And Flimby's in the closet,
Cos its misunderstood.

For only Flimby people know,
Only they can see,
That our home deserves the name,
Of 'Flimby by the Sea.'

Two People

Two people, out there,
Somewhere, on the earth.
Enter the world,
On the day of their birth.
Parents and siblings,
Friends and relations,
All come together,
For life's new creation.
A baby to cherish,
An angel to love.
Sent from the spirit,
Somewhere above.
They laugh and they cry,
They feed and they grow.
Blossom, develop
And learn as they go.
From baby to childhood,
Then childhood is gone.
In the blink of an eye,
They've turned 21.
Now life is for living,
Places to go.
Somewhere to be
And someone to know.
For now, they are young,
They are single and free.
But one day they realise,
One day they see,

Each day is important,
A story, untold,
Life is for sharing
And love is the goal.
They send out a vibe,
They don't even know,
It's telling their soul,
It's time to come home,
The universe listens,
Majestic and clever,
She puts things in place,
To bring them together.
Unaware of the magic,
They head to the night.
They meet in the music
And something feels right.
They're chatting , they're flirting,
They're playing the game.
The circle of life is starting again.
They look to each other
And somehow they see,
That "I am in you."
And "You are in me."
They open their heart,
They're taking a chance.
Two people in love
Begin a new dance.
They know in their heart
That this is for life,
That he'll be her husband.

And she'll be his wife.
He's taking his time,
He's put to the test.
But he know he just wants
To give her the best.
To Paris they travel,
He bends on one knee
And hopefully asks,
"Will you marry me?"
No need to ask,
No need to guess.
Her answer is simple,
"It's always been yes.
Always been you,
From the day that we met.
The person who knows me
And fits me the best."
Now, for a wedding,
A day full of joy,
To capture the love
Of a girl and a boy.
To look to the future,
Remember the past,
For life is a river,
That travels so fast.
It carries us forward,
It twists and turns,
With every new challenge,
We grow and we learn.
But now, we are here

And they stand, face to face.
Ignoring life's madness,
Forgetting its pace.
A moment in time,
Two hearts entwined,
I'll always be yours,
You'll always be mine.
Locked in a gaze,
As they stand together.
They smile for they know,
They are seeing forever.

Chapter 2 - Two People in Love

Two people in love,
Alone in the dark.
A kiss and a cuddle,
A magical spark.
Anticipation,
A little white stick.
Two blue lines,
Feel a bit sick.
Tears of joy,
A little round tummy.
Will we have enough space?
Will we have enough money?
9 month pass,
The day has arrived.
Cramps and contractions.
He's there, by your side.
Pain and frustration.
Blood sweat and tears.
One final push.
Your baby is here.
A miracles happened,
Everything's changed.
You've fallen in love,
You're choosing a name.
Time to go home.
What do we do?
House full of chaos,
Tired, confused.

Dirty nappies,
Sleepless nights,
Early mornings,
Not so bright.
Washing and changing,
Bottles and baths.
Tears and tantrums,
Giggles and laughs.
Being a clown,
Acting a fool.
First smile,
First steps,
Then first day at school.
They make you feel happy,
They make you feel sad.
They tell you they love you,
Then treat you so bad.
There's ups and there's downs,
There's highs and there's lows.
Drying a tear, wiping a nose,
Bedtime stories, Christmas Day,
Fun to have,
Games to play.
Clothes too short,
Growing and growing.
Money keeps churning,
Love keeps flowing.
Family gets bigger,
Time passes on,
Childhood is over,

Where have the years gone?
Hormones and mood swings,
Slamming of doors.
Ignoring their parents,
Avoiding their chores.
Need independence,
Like their own space.
Start to cut ties,
Friends take your place.
Time to move on,
Time to move out,
"If we need anything.
We'll give you a shout."
Eerie silence,
Nothings the same.
The children are gone,
But the memories remain.
One empty house,
Two heavy hearts,
Beating together,
Alone in the dark.
You've done your job,
They've flown the nest.
Time to yourself,
Solitude, rest.
You start to feel better,
It's not as it seems,
They're out in the world,
Achieving their dreams.
One day they come knocking,

With husband or wife.
"We've made something special,
Created a life.
Your grandchild is coming,"
You laugh and you cry.
You promise to help them,
And be by their side.
Your story continues,
Onward it flows,
A river of love,
It grows and it grows.
Shining its light,
Cutting its course,
The next generation
Feeling its force.
Old age is here,
But, you know that it's fair.
The wrinkles don't matter.
The love is still there.
Alone in the dark,
You lie face to face,
In this infinite ocean,
Of matter and space.
Two people in love,
Two souls together,
Content, for you know,
That love lasts forever.

Moments

There are moments in life that we treasure.
They are gone in the blink of an eye.
So precious they cannot be measured.
Too costly for money to buy.

The joy in the face of a baby.
The warmth of the sweet summer sun.
The sound of the birds in the morning,
As they tell us that Springtime has come.

A gaze and a smile from our soul mate,
A laugh and a joke with a friend.
An end of night dance, to our favourite song,
When we know that the party must end.

We must cherish each day as it greets us.
As we go on this journey, together.
Capture the laughter, bottle the smiles,
And remember the moments forever.

Girl

I'm a complicated, simple girl.
My dreams are big and small.
I'm everything I want to be,
Yet not myself at all.
I'm as sad as I am happy
And as weak as I am strong.
I could cry through all the good times.
Then laugh when things go wrong.
I'm a walking contradiction.
Confused and pleased to be.
I think I've finally found myself.
I'm everything. I'm me.

To My Children

May the sun shine upon you and make you feel whole.

May the moonlight caress you and nurture your soul.

May the soft summer rain wash your worries away.

May the gentle winds blow inspiration your way.

May you wake every day with a song in your heart

And a spring in your step on each journey you start.

May you follow the rainbow through trouble and strife.

May you know how I love you, each day of your life.

Higher Consciousness

Open your heart with good intentions,
Believe in more than three dimensions.
Uncover the lock and find the key,
Open the door, your mind is free.

Lose your 'self' and see your soul,
We are not one, we are a whole.
Water, fire, earth and sky
Again, we're born, we live, we die.

The physical world is just a game,
Reality's on a higher plane.
A web of life, a living sea,
A wave, a thought, a frequency.

When will is free, you have a choice,
To hear the word of the higher voice
And try to understand the notion,
Of how to overcome emotion.

Every thought creates a vibe,
Starts a ripple, forms a tide.
And always comes around again,
Returns the love, inflicts the pain.

Somewhere deep inside your mind,
A seed exists for you to find.
Nurture it and it will grow.
Affecting everything you know.

A positive thought, a loving deed,
A simple smile, you've sown the seed.
Know the rules, problem solved.
And thus your spirit has evolved.

Knowledge, wisdom, love divine,
Your inner light begins to shine.
Seek to know your higher self.
If you have this, then you have wealth.

Allow yourself to just believe,
In life beyond what you perceive.
Dare to look and you will see,
A secret door that sets you free.

Consciousness is all that's real,
The way we think and act and feel,
Creates the world we see as true,
A world that can be changed by you.

Be good and giving, fair and kind
And quickly you will start to find,
It's not so hard to change the day,
Of other souls who pass your way.

And what you give you will receive,
Allow yourself to just believe.
Live your life for the greater cause,
And the meaning of life,
Will then be yours.

The Light

Even in my darkest hour,
I know the dawn will come.
Look behind the storm clouds
And I'll always find the Sun.

So when the world is heavy,
And I feel I've lost my sight.
I know it's fine,
It's simply time,
To look towards the light.

Mum

My closest friend, my guiding light,
The one who loves me, wrong or right.
You've shared my troubles, dried my tears,
Gave advice to calm my fears.

Throughout the years, I've always known,
I never have to feel alone.
For you were there to take my hand,
And make me feel you understand.

So now I'd like to help you see,
That all the love you gave to me,
Has made me happy, made me strong,
Taught me how to get along.

I'd like to take the time today,
To thank you for each precious day,
You gave your all and I am blessed.
I love you Mum, you are the best.

Dad

On the day that I was born,
I know you shed a tear.
You had what you wanted,
Your little girl was here.

You promised to take care of me,
And always be around.
Dad, you've kept that promise,
You've never let me down.

The first man I looked up to,
Dependable and strong,
A person I could turn to,
When things in life went wrong.

You taught me how to think big thoughts,
And question what is true,
My curious, deep nature,
Was passed on down from you.

You always put your faith in me,
And let me find my path,
Although at times I lost my way,
Your guidance brought me back.

And every day you loved me,
Unconsciously, I planned,
What I'd look for in a husband,
When I grew and found a man.

No matter what life throws at me.
On you, I can depend,
You'll always be my hero,
My Dad, my rock, my friend.

Our First Born Child

Our baby, our child,
You're here at last.
But time keeps on ticking
And passes so fast.

We watch you in wonder,
So bright and so clever.
Desperate to capture,
Each moment forever.

Your curious eyes,
Your innocent face,
Seeing the world,
As a magical place.

Your early bird smile
Has a magical way,
Of setting the mood
For the rest of the day.

Life is so different,
A new point of view.
Nothing else matters,
But caring for you.

Hearing your laughter,
Drying your tears,
Seeing you smiling,
Calming your fears.

We live and we breathe,
For your kisses and hugs,
Your smiles are out weakness,
Your laughter our drug.

Life is more simple,
Loving and giving.
You gave us our purpose,
Our reason for living.

Our bond is eternal,
So pure and so true.
Nothing can make us,
As proud as you do.

Our baby, our child,
Our gift from above,
We'll always be here,
With infinite love.

Little Clouds (inspired by Wordsworth)

I wandered lonely as a cloud,
That floats on high o'vale and hill.
Then I saw another cloud,
And I was calm and still.

I'd drifted through a thousand skies,
Through many of life's storms,
And came across so many clouds,
In many other forms.

But you were somehow, different.
Inside, we were the same.
And so we floated onwards,
To sunshine and to rain.

No matter what life threw at us,
No matter what the weather,
We stayed within each other's sight
And always stuck together.

Our love was pure and simple,
Our bond was firm and strong.
And in a moving, changing world
We gently merged as one.

Our everlasting journey,
Together we would fly.
Dancing on the winds of change.
Through life's eternal skies.

One Soul

You left me there at the gateway,
You kissed me and said your goodbyes.
You promised me that you would see me again.
You told me that love never dies.

I watched as you entered the tunnel,
And followed the pure white light.
The last thing I saw was your shadow,
I stood there alone in the night.

And slowly I started forgetting,
That I was now half of a soul,
I always knew something was missing,
That somehow, I wasn't quite whole.

I followed the light to this lifetime,
I entered the physical dream.
I wandered into an existence,
Where nothing is quite as it seems.

But somehow I knew you were out there,
In the infinite ocean of space.
A brand new reality started,
But I couldn't remember your face.

It would have been easy to lose you,
But destiny gave us a way.
With a bolt of divine interception,
We came back together one day.

I lost myself in your charisma,
The attraction was second to none.
I began to see why I had met you,
I understood you were the one.

We know we can never be parted,
Eternity lies at our feet.
The universe carves our journey,
And will always ensure that we meet.

Our souls will continue evolving,
Living and growing together.
And each time I look in your beautiful eyes,
I'll know that I'm seeing forever.

To My Unborn Baby

To the life that's inside me,
I've solemnly sworn,
To love and protect you,
My precious unborn.

Each day I ask questions,
As I feel you grow.
Where will you get to?
Who will you know?

What will you look like,
Daughter or son?
Just like your Daddy?
Or more like your Mum?

Will you be caring?
Will you be shy?
Will you be funny,
Your confidence high?

A doctor, a painter?
No matter to me,
As long as you're happy,
Contented and free.

Although you're inside me,
It's easy to see
That you are a person,
Just waiting to be.

To look and to listen,
To work and to earn,
To grow and develop,
To love and to learn.

I've day dreamed about you
And time goes so fast.
A few months from now,
I will meet you at last.

My baby, my child,
My gift to the earth,
In anticipation,
I wait for your birth.

Imagine

Imagine me and I'll be with you,
Talk to me and I'll pass by.
I exist in a place that's eternal,
In the moon and the stars and the sky.

You may think that I'm no longer here.
But death is a word that's untrue.
My consciousness flies, though infinite skies
And I am still living, in you.

All of the things that I taught you,
Came from my spirit, you see.
I raised you with all of my virtues,
So you are an image of me.

So while you are grieving, remember,
My spirit is helping you heal.
Imagine me and I'll be with you.
For what you imagine, is real.

Our Family is Complete

Our hearts were filed with endless joy,
The day we had our baby boy.
The little man we longed to meet,
He came and made our life complete.

We almost knew that he was there,
We felt his spirit, said a prayer
And wished upon a shining star,
For one of each, how blessed we are.

Our gorgeous girl, our first born child,
An only one for quite a while.
She always hoped we'd have another,
Now she has her little brother.

To see him grin and watch him play,
To hear him giggle makes our day.
His smiling eyes, his cheerful face.
He's made our home a better place.

And so we thank the heavens above,
For all the laughter, all the love
And the joy we've ever felt.
A marvellous hand we have been dealt.

We gave them life and with their birth,
We leave our mark on planet earth.
So here we stand, Husband and Wife.
To thank you God for our life.

Forever grateful we will stay,
For the little ones you sent our way,
For all the memories yet to make,
All adventures yet to take.

And all the love that's yet to give,
Each and every day they live.

Two little trees

If you and I were little trees,
Fresh and green and new,
I think I would be planted,
In a place right next to you.

Some nurture and some tenderness,
Would then be quite essential,
In helping us two tiny trees,
Reach our full potential.

And as we grew together,
To keep our love alive,
We'd need to feed each other
And help each other thrive.

We'd share a daily tonic,
Of love and sweet affection,
To stop our growing branches,
From taking new directions.

Without a little nurture
A tree will start to die,
Its weak and tired branches,
Will never touch the sky.

You and I are little trees,
Growing strong together.
I think our roots are so deep now,
That we'll be here forever.

Mother Earth

Mother Earth was weary,
And feeling rather sad.
Her kids took her for granted,
And treated her so bad.

She gave them such a lovely home,
A haven they could cherish.
But yet they seemed oblivious,
As she began to perish.

She let them make their own mistakes,
She watched them misbehave.
She cried as they just turned their back,
On all the love she gave.

They scattered her with rubbish,
Polluted her with greed.
Ignored her gentle cries for help,
And all her simple needs.

Then one day, she had had enough.
Her mood began to turn,
"If I don't start to stand my ground,"
"My children will not learn."

As they tore her forests down,
She felt her lungs collapse.
She turned up all her thermostats,
And switched on all her taps.

She sent some mighty tremors,
Across her damaged core.
She cried out to her children,
"I can't take anymore".

And all the clever children,
Began to see their fate.
They knew that if they changed their ways.
It still, was not too late.

Let's hope the clever children,
The ones who use their voice,
Can make the other children see
That we don't have a choice.

We have to love our Mother Earth,
We have to pull together,
To keep her clean and safe from harm,
So she'll be here forever.

No Tomorrow

If I knew there was no tomorrow,
The end of our time together,
I would capture your laughter,
And lock up your voice,
And play it back forever.

If I knew you would be going,
And leaving me behind,
I'd take an image of your face,
And carve it on my mind.

If I knew I couldn't hold you,
And the next kiss was the last,
I'd gather a thousand memories,
And linger in the past.

Tomorrow is never a promise.
We assume it will come our way.
And forget what really matters,
In the issues of the day.

But every day is precious,
And time is always borrowed.
Let's try to always live and love,
As if there was no tomorrow.

Daily Prayer

I call upon my higher self
And ask that you ignite,
Divine and pure protection,
With a ray of golden light.

Let the light surround me,
All throughout the day,
Blocking negativity,
That may be sent my way.

Let the light dissolve my fears.
The light of all creation.
Leaving only higher thoughts
To raise my own vibration.

Our love will bring us back together

You may not be able to hear me,
You maybe can't see that I'm there.
But I'm always above and around you,
In your heart, through your love and your prayer.

I know that you're sad and you'll miss me,
But I want you to smile as you think,
Of our precious and magical memories,
For our lives pass us by in a blink.

We are lucky we had one another,
We are lucky for all we achieved,
We are lucky for all of the times that we shared.
And all of the love we received.

Our love is a force, never ending.
So strong it can overcome pain.
And all of the boundaries that part us at death,
So we can be together again.

Polarity

Without the low, there is no high,
Cannot laugh if we don't cry.
Can't feel joy if we don't feel pain,
The sun is void if there is no rain.
Darkness lets us see the light.
Where is day without the night?
Tragedy, romance, a bittersweet tale,
We grow, we fall, succeed and fail.
And as we walk, we start to see,
It was always simply, meant to be.
Moments that were there to cherish,
Pain that proved we would not perish.
The cycle of life, a beautiful game.
Like the changing seasons, starts again,
Perfect in its every way.,
Whatever comes, you'll be ok.

Solway Skies

One day I'll walk to the end of the earth,
And gaze at the view to value its worth.
I think I'll find with no surprise,
It cannot match the Solway skies.

A view, of which, I'll never tire.
The ever changing amber fires,
Sunsets where we shared a kiss,
Indigo and ocean mists.

And Criffel but a silhouette,
On a palette which is never set.
I look to her when times are tough,
And her seas are calm, or wild and rough.

My heart swells with appreciation,
She gives me hope and inspiration.
A companion, who, through toil and strife,
Reminds me of the gift of life.

When I reach my end of days,
And the breath of life begins to fade.
And memories rise to sooth my mind,
She'll be there, profound, sublime.

In setting Sun , with shadows casting,
I'll see that life is everlasting.
I'll lie, at peace and close my eyes
And give my soul, to the Solway Skies.

For more poetry, to order more copies of my book or a bespoke poem, please visit my Facebook page.

www.facebook.com/wordybird73

Or alternatively, go to Lulu.com and search for

'Solway Skies'

Love and Light xx

Wordybird xx